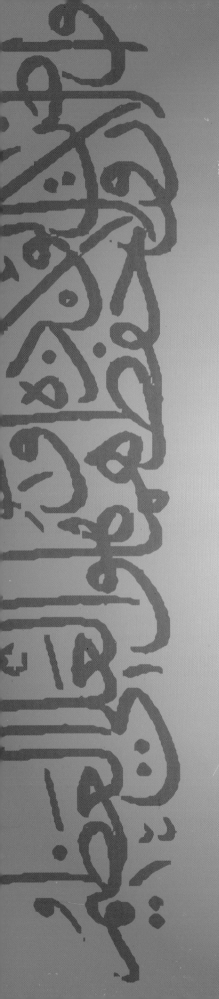

WORLD RELIGIONS

Islam

Richard Tames

W
FRANKLIN WATTS
LONDON·SYDNEY

This edition 2005

J
297

Franklin Watts
96 Leonard Street
London, EC2A 4XD

Franklin Watts Australia
Level 17/207 Kent Street
Sydney, NSW 2000

© Franklin Watts 1999

Editor: Sarah Snashall
Art director: Robert Walster
Designer: Simon Borrough
Picture research: Sue Mennell
Religious Consultants: Nazar Mustafa,
Education Advisor, Islamic Cultural Centre,
Regent's Park Mosque
Angela Wood, teacher, broadcaster and
curriculum adviser in religious education
Lesley Prior, Advisory teacher and lecturer
in religious education

A CIP catalogue record for this book is
available from the British Library.

ISBN 0 7496 6420 7

Dewey classification 297

Printed in China

Picture credits:

Cover photographs:
Peter Sanders (right); Christine
Osborne Pictures (inset)

AKG London p. 13b
Robert Harding Picture Library pp. 11
(Simon Harris), 13t, 16 (Simon
Westcott), 23b
Impact Photos pp. 7b (Mark Henley),
29b (Christophe Bluntzer)
Hutchison Library pp. 15b (Gerard),
18b (Sarah Errington)
Christine Osborne Pictures pp. 5b,
17t, 18t, 19, 22t, 22b, 23t
Panos Pictures pp. 12 (John Spaull),
27b (Jean-Leo Dugast)
Peter Sanders pp. 4, 6, 7t, 8, 9t, 9b, 14,
15t, 20, 21t, 21b, 24t, 24-25, 26, 27t
R.L. Tames p. 5t
Trip Photo Library pp. 17b, 29t
(Helene Rogers)

maps pp.10, 28 Julian Baker

When a Muslim uses the name of
Allah or the Prophet Muhammad, they
show respect by saying, 'Peace and
blessings be upon Him'.

CONTENTS

ONE GOD

ISLAM IS AN ARABIC WORD which means 'submitting'. A Muslim is a follower of Islam and someone who promises to submit to Allah.

Prophets

Muslims believe that throughout history, Allah (God) has sent prophets to tell people the meaning of life and how to live it. The first prophet was Adam and the last was the Prophet Muhammad. Islam respects many prophets of Judaism and Christianity, including Ibrahim (Abraham), Musa (Moses) and Isa (Jesus). Muslims believe that Allah's final revelation sums up and makes clear all the teachings of previous prophets. It was revealed to the Prophet Muhammad and is recorded in the Qur'an.

The Pillars of Islam

Muslims have five basic duties:
1. To say the Shahadah, the declaration of faith, which states that Allah is the only god and that the Prophet Muhammad is his messenger.
2. To pray five times a day.
3. To give zakat (money to charity).
4. To fast during daylight in the month of Ramadan.
5. To go on a pilgrimage to Makkah.

This image of a praying man is created out of the words of the Shahadah.

Unity and diversity

Muslims believe that Allah is the creator of the universe, invisible and eternal. Allah is a single being, more powerful, more loving and more wise than any human could imagine.

There are Muslims throughout the world. They speak different languages, but they are united by the same basic beliefs and duties. They all use Arabic as the language of prayer and pray facing towards Makkah.

'No mortal eyes can see Him, though He sees all eyes, He is kind and all-knowing.'

Qur'an 6 : 103

Life and death

Muslims believe that every human being is born without sin. A Muslim can then choose to follow Allah's teachings or to disobey them and do evil. After death, Allah will judge each individual and send them to heaven or hell, depending on how they have lived their lives.

Zakat

Zakat is one of the Pillars of Islam. It is given once a year, and is calculated as 2.5 per cent of someone's surplus wealth (savings, and jewellery that is not worn).

A Muslim gives zakat.

Becoming a Muslim

Anyone can be a Muslim. An adult can become a Muslim by reciting the declaration of faith, called the Shahadah, in front of two adult Muslim witnesses. Most people, however, are born into Islam.

Birth

When a baby is born, the father may whisper the Shahadah, the declaration of faith, into the baby's ear. When the baby is a week old, its head may be shaved as a sign of newness. The baby is then named. Sometimes an animal is sacrificed in celebration and one-third of the animal is eaten by the family and the rest is given to the poor. A male child will be circumcised, although in some Muslim countries this may take place when the child is older.

A father whispers the Shahadah into the ear of his new-born child.

'I witness that there is no god but Allah and that Muhammad is the Prophet of Allah.'

The Shahadah

Growing in faith

From their earliest years, Muslim children see their parents pray at home and are encouraged to join in. From about seven, the children will begin to fast during Ramadan.

An adult convert to Islam makes the declaration of faith before two adult witnesses.

The same but different

A mosque is a centre for worship, study and social activities in an Islamic community. Each mosque is independent, but all Muslims think of themselves as belonging to the ummah, the world-wide community of believers. There are, however, different traditions of worship. Most Muslims are Sunnis, followers of the Sunna (example) of the Prophet Muhammad. Some Muslims are Shi'a Muslims, who follow the guidance of the Prophet Muhammad's son-in-law, Ali, as well.

Religion and daily life

Muslims believe the Prophet Muhammad's life and example show how to make Islam the framework of daily life. The Pillars of Islam are all-powerful reminders of a Muslim's daily duty to Allah and the community.

These Muslim girls live in China. Muslims make up only a minority of China's population, but there are still 50 million of them.

The Last Prophet

THE PROPHET MUHAMMAD WAS BORN IN MAKKAH, a trading city in Arabia in the Middle East, around 570CE. At 25, he was a rich and respected merchant. He could have had an easy life. Instead he worried about the evils he saw around him.

Revelation

The Prophet Muhammad meditated in a cave on Mount Hira, outside Makkah. One day in 610 he heard a voice commanding him to recite the words he heard. At first he feared that he was going mad. But the voice returned repeatedly, speaking in beautiful verse, convincing the Prophet Muhammad that Allah was using an angel to communicate with him.

The cave on Mount Hira where Muslims believe the Prophet first heard the angel Jibril (Gabriel) reciting Allah's word.

Recite in the name of Allah who created, Created man from a clot of blood. Recite!

Qur'an 96 : 1

In 613 he began to spread the messages he had received. His wife and some of his relatives accepted him as a true prophet. The beautiful poetry of the message the Prophet was reciting convinced others that the message was indeed sent from Allah. But the wealthy rulers of Makkah resented his preaching against injustice, greed, gambling, drunkenness and the worshipping of idols.

Migration and unity

In 622 the Prophet Muhammad and his followers left Makkah to live in Madinah, where the local people had invited him to be their judge. War broke out between the people of Makkah and the people of Madinah. Tribes from the surrounding area came to pledge loyalty to the Prophet Muhammad and his teachings.

In 630 the Prophet Muhammad returned in triumph to Makkah as its ruler. He cleared the idols from the sacred building in Makkah called the Ka'aba and forbade Muslims to fight each other. When the Prophet Muhammad died in 632, Arabia was more peaceful and united than it had ever been.

Muslims pray towards the Ka'aba in Makkah.

Messenger and example

Muslims do not believe that the Prophet Muhammad was divine, but they believe his message was. His sayings and example provide a model of how Muslims should behave in all areas of their lives.

The Great Mosque of the Prophet Muhammad in Madinah.

THE SPREAD OF ISLAM

WHEN THE PROPHET Muhammad died, some of the Arab tribes that had followed him broke away from Islam. Muslim armies were sent against them. Muslims would not allow other Muslims to give up their religion.

This map shows the expansion of the area under Muslim rule in the centuries after the death of the Prophet Muhammad.

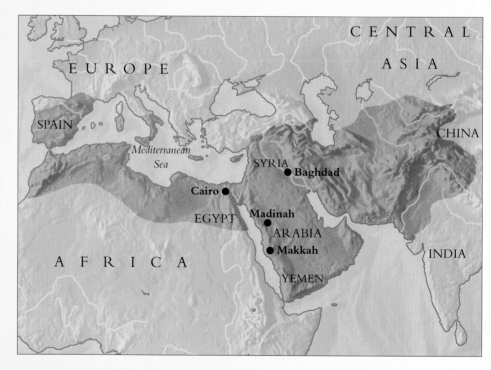

Expansion

Muslim expeditions against disloyal tribes became a war to expand Muslim territory. Soon Muslims clashed with the great neighbouring empires of Byzantium and Persia. These empires had been weakened by long wars with each other and the Muslim armies were able to defeat them. In many cities, Muslims were welcomed because they promised to bring peace, order, lighter taxes and respect for other religions.

Muslims took over the whole Persian empire and the rich Byzantine provinces of Syria and Egypt. Further conquests were made until Muslim territories stretched from Spain to the borders of India. Muslim merchants even carried the faith as far as China. Baghdad in Iraq, built between 758 and 762, became the Muslim world's greatest centre of government, trade and learning.

Many rulers – same rules

By then it had become impossible to rule all the lands of Islam from a single centre. In distant regions like Spain and Yemen local rulers increasingly ignored Baghdad. In 1258 and again in 1401, Baghdad was attacked by Mongol armies from Central Asia. The eastern lands of Islam were badly devastated and Cairo in Egypt became the greatest city of Islam.

The Alhambra palace at Granada, in Spain. It was the last outpost of Muslim rule in Spain, which ended in 1492.

Although Muslim lands were split among different rulers they all upheld an Islamic code of laws. Arabic remained the language of government and religion. Its spread enabled scholars, pilgrims and traders to travel easily throughout the lands of Islam.

ART AND SCIENCE

ISLAM CREATED NEW AND DISTINCTIVE kinds of art and architecture. Muslim scholars also made important advances in science and medicine.

Art in Islam

The Prophet Muhammad preached against the worship of idols made of wood or stone. Because of this, there are no statues or pictures to be seen in a mosque, and Muslims do not make pictures of any of the prophets or early Islamic leaders. Instead Muslims developed their own particular approach to religious art, using patterns made from mathematical or plant shapes, or beautiful writing of verses from the Qur'an. These represent the order of the universe, the beauty and richness of Allah's creation and the lasting truths of the teachings of the Qur'an.

Traditionally, Muslim artists never signed their work. This expressed their belief that they were simply reflecting Allah's creation – not acting as creators themselves.

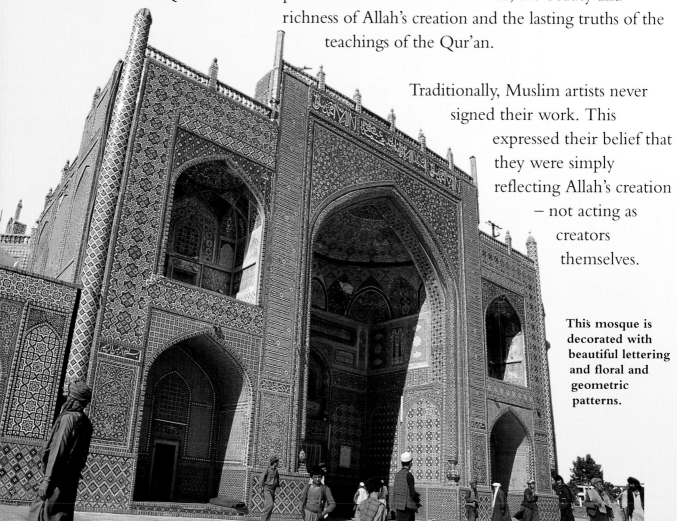

This mosque is decorated with beautiful lettering and floral and geometric patterns.

Science in Islam

Practical religious problems, such as the need to find the direction of Makkah when they prayed and to calculate the calendar, led Muslims to excel in mathematics and astronomy. Because Muslims believe in the resurrection of the body on the day of judgement, Muslim doctors were traditionally unwilling to use surgery except as a last resort. So they became expert in curing people with medicine, diet, sleep, exercise and massage. Islam's stress on washing before prayer made doctors aware of the value of personal hygiene.

Muslim scholars observing the stars and planets. Muslim scholars were expert at astronomy. Many stars still have Arabic names.

Doctors in a garden of herbs and healing plants. These were made into medicines and ointments.

Because the Prophet Muhammad encouraged his followers to 'seek knowledge, even as far as China', Muslim scholars preserved the learning of the ancient Greeks. It was mostly through Arabic translations coming through Muslim-ruled Spain that Christian Europe regained a knowledge of Greek achievements in mathematics, medicine and science.

'It was He that gave the sun his brightness and the moon her light, ordering her phases that you may learn to calculate the seasons and the years.'

Qur'an 10 : 5

THE QUR'AN

THE QUR'AN, the holy book of the Muslims, records all the revelations to the Prophet Muhammad. It plays a central part in the life of a Muslim, telling him or her how to live their life and worship Allah.

Revealed by Allah

Muslims believe that the Qur'an records Allah's words, not the Prophet Muhammad's. The first revealed passage of the Qur'an was Allah's command to pass on what Allah told the Prophet Muhammad to say.

The Qur'an is divided into 114 Surahs (chapters). Some are rich with poetic language, describing the wonders of the universe, the beauties of heaven and the horrors of hell. The beauty of these passages convinced many early Muslims that they must be Allah's words because no human poet could have written them. Other, longer, chapters deal with historical events and Allah's law.

Because the Qur'an represents Allah's own words, copies of the Qur'an are often beautifully decorated and bound.

A Muslim boy studies the Qur'an.

A book to recite

In Muslim countries important public ceremonies, meetings, conferences and family celebrations usually begin with someone reciting passages from the Qur'an. A Muslim who knows the entire Qur'an by heart is known as a hafiz. This has traditionally been an occupation for blind people who could use their skill to earn an honourable living from reciting passages on public occasions.

The Qur'an may be translated into other languages for study, but only the Arabic original is used for worship – even though most Muslims don't speak Arabic as their first language.

A Muslim studies the Qur'an in the quiet of a mosque.

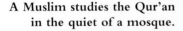

Law and tradition

The Qur'an contains many laws for Muslims. The other great source of Islamic law is the Hadith (tradition), the record of the Prophet Muhammad's actions and sayings. The Qur'an, for example, tells Muslims to pray – the Hadith tells them how.

The cover and the pages of this copy of the Qur'an are decorated with patterns in gold paint.

A PLACE OF WORSHIP

THE MOSQUE is the most important building in a Muslim community and often serves as a school, a library and a meeting-hall as well as for worship. Some mosques are among the world's most beautiful buildings, but a mosque can be very simple.

The mosque

Muslims may pray to Allah anywhere as long as the ground is clean. However, adult male Muslims should go to a mosque to pray together just after midday on Fridays. Walls are needed to separate the mosque from its surroundings and create a calm area away from busy markets, traffic and other distractions. There must be a pool, fountain, tank or taps to provide water for washing, and somewhere to hold shoes.

This mosque is in Pakistan. The courtyard can hold many people on festival days.

There should be a covered area, preferably carpeted, where worshippers can assemble in orderly rows. Usually a mosque has a tower called a minaret from which a muezzin calls people to prayer.

Mosques are built so that worshippers pray in the direction of Makkah. Inside the covered part of the mosque, there is usually a mark or niche, called a mihrab, on one wall to indicate this direction. In larger mosques there is often a minbar (pulpit) as well.

A muezzin calls Muslims to prayer. Nowadays, a tape-recording is often used.

'Whoever builds a mosque, desiring thereby Allah's pleasure, Allah builds the same for him in paradise.'

A traditional saying of Muhammad

The imam

There are no priests in Islam, but larger mosques have an imam who leads the prayers of the congregation and, on Fridays, preaches the sermon. The sermon either explains some aspect of Islamic faith or history, or discusses a current issue from the religious point of view. Often the imam will also be an expert in Islamic law, able to serve as a judge.

The imam stands on a minbar to give his Friday sermon. In this mosque, the minbar is a finely-carved staircase.

PRAYER

MUSLIMS SHOULD PRAY FIVE TIMES A DAY – before sunrise, after midday, in late afternoon, after sunset and in the evening. Through words and actions, the worshipper expresses praise, gratitude, submission, a desire for forgiveness and fellowship with others.

Preparing to pray

Before praying, called salah, a Muslim must first announce his or her intention to pray, called niyyah. After niyyah, a Muslim performs wudu (washing): a Muslim washes his or her face, ears, nose, mouth, hands, arms and feet.

A Muslims performs wudu (left).

A Muslim prays in the desert (below).

Praying

A Muslim prays using a set series of words and movements, called a rak'ah, which is repeated two to four times, depending on the time of day:

1 The worshipper makes the statement of faith.

2 Standing upright, the worshipper, with palms raised, declares *'Allah is great'*.

3 With folded hands the worshipper recites the opening passage of the Qur'an:

'Praise be to Allah Lord of the Universe, the Merciful, the Mercy giving!

Ruler of the Day for Repayment!

You alone we worship and to You alone we turn for help.

Guide us on the straight path,

The path of those You have favoured,

With whom You are not angry nor who are lost.'

4 Bending from the hips, the worshipper says three times, *'Glory be to my Great Lord and praise be to Him.'*

5 Standing, the worshipper says, *'Allah listens to those who thank Him, O Lord thanks be to You.'*

6 The worshipper kneels, with hands and forehead to the ground, saying, *'Glory be to my Lord, the Most High, Allah is greater than all else.'*

7 Kneeling, with palms on knees, the worshipper three times says, *'O my Master, forgive me.'*

8 Step 6 is repeated.

9 The final rak'ah ends as worshippers look right and left, saying to each other, *'Peace be with you and the mercy of Allah.'*

A man kneels with his hands on his knees to pray.

FOOD AND FASTING

MUSLIMS HAVE STRICT RULES ABOUT EATING. In keeping these rules, they show their devotion to Allah.

A Muslim mother visits a halal butcher. The meat sold in the shop is from animals that have been killed in the correct way.

Halal and haram

Food that Muslims can eat and activities that they can do are called halal (permitted). Most kinds of fish and fresh vegetables are permitted to Muslims. For meat to be halal, the animal must be killed in a special way. The butcher must declare that he is killing the animal in Allah's name to show that he is taking life for human benefit. Afterwards, the animal must be drained of blood before it is eaten. Animals dying of disease or an accident may not be eaten.

Some food cannot be eaten by Muslims, these foods are called haram (forbidden). Alcohol is haram – the Qur'an says that it robs people of their normal good sense. Drinking alcohol can lead to quarrels and violence. Other foods that are haram are meat from pigs, rodents, reptiles or meat-eating animals.

Muslims should thank Allah for their food both before they start a meal and after they have finished it.

Fasting

During the month of Ramadan, the month in which Muhammad first began to receive revelations from Allah, Muslims do not eat or drink at all during the hours of daylight. This sawm (fast) helps to develop self-control, prevent greediness and remind everyone of the hunger of the very poor.

A Muslim family gathers in the dark to eat during the month of fasting.

Children under twelve and very old people are excused from fasting. Women expecting or breast-feeding a baby, people who are sick and travellers on a journey are allowed to eat but should make up the days they missed by fasting later on. In many Muslim countries restaurants and cafés close during daylight hours. After the muezzin calls for evening prayer, eating is again permitted.

There are many ways that the beginning and end of the fast is announced, such as by a bulletin on the radio and television, a drummer or a cannon.

In some Muslim communities a gun is fired to signal to people when daylight has ended and they can have a meal.

FESTIVALS

THERE ARE MANY FESTIVALS IN THE MUSLIM CALENDAR. The most important are Id-ul-Fitr which marks the end of the fasting of Ramadan, and Id-ul-Adha which celebrates Allah's intervention in Ibrahim's sacrifice of his son.

Arab men dance in celebration of Id-ul-Fitr.

Muslims flock to a park in Cairo, Egypt, to celebrate Id-ul-Fitr.

Id-ul-Fitr

Id-ul-Fitr marks the end of fasting through the month of Ramadan. To thank Allah for being allowed to end their fasting, Muslims give zakat to the poor and for good causes.

To mark this special occasion, Muslims bathe, put on new clothes and wear perfume. After prayers at the mosque, families gather for a feast and eat special sweets. It is also a time for visiting family and friends. This often includes a visit to the cemetery so that dead members of the family are also remembered. People also send out greeting cards which say 'Id Mabarak' ('have a blessed festival').

Thousands of Muslims gather at a mosque to pray during a festival.

A boy holds a lamb which will be killed and the meat given to the poor.

Id-ul-Adha

This festival coincides with the pilgrimage to Makkah and is celebrated on the tenth day of the month of Dhu'l-hijjah. Id-ul-Adha recalls the story of Prophet Ibrahim who was called by Allah to sacrifice his son as a test of faith and obedience. At the last minute, Allah provided a ram for sacrifice instead.

At Id-ul-Adha, some Muslim families buy and slaughter a sheep, goat or cow as a symbol of their obedience to Allah. One-third of the meat is kept by them for their own use and the rest is given away to the poor. This Id, too, is marked by family gatherings and feasting.

23

PILGRIMAGE TO MAKKAH

ONCE IN A LIFETIME, every healthy adult Muslim should go on a pilgrimage, call hajj, to Makkah. Afterwards a man can add the title Hajji to his name; a woman can add the title Hajjah.

A spiritual state

Between the 7th and 10th of Dhu'l-hijjah, the 12th month of the Islamic calendar, two million Muslims meet in Makkah. As they arrive they enter a state known as ihram. Men wear two white, unsewn cotton sheets, one around the waist, the other over the shoulder. Women wear a long, plain dress and head-covering, but may not wear a veil.

Pilgrims gather at Mina to throw pebbles at stone pillars as a symbol that they reject the devil.

Dressing the same shows that all believers are equal in Allah's sight. The pilgrims may not use perfume, wear jewellery, cut their hair or nails, have any sexual relations or kill any living thing.

Rituals to remember

At Makkah, pilgrims perform rituals and prayers recalling special aspects of Islam. They walk seven times anti-clockwise round the Ka'aba. Then they visit the well of ZamZam and walk seven times between the two small hills of Marwa and Safa in memory of Hagar, wife of Ibrahim. Hagar had searched there for water for her son, Ismail, and found ZamZam through Allah's mercy.

The pilgrims then go to the plain of Arafat where the Prophet Muhammad preached his last sermon. Here they stand praying from noon until sunset. For most of the year, this place is an empty desert. But for one day it becomes a temporary city of two million people. Next the pilgrims go to the village of Mina to throw stones at three stone pillars to symbolize rejecting the devil. Finally, after sacrificing a sheep or camel, they go round the Ka'aba again.

Pilgrims walking round the Ka'aba. This acknowledges the Ka'aba as the focus of prayer.

THE FAMILY AND ISLAM

MUSLIMS BELIEVE FAMILY LIFE IS ESSENTIAL for everyone. Islam does not approve of people living alone. Orphans and old people left on their own should be looked after as part of a family. Muslims think it would be shameful for a member of their family to be sent to live in an old people's home.

Marriage

In many Muslim countries people marry after an agreement between their families rather than simply because they have fallen in love. Arranged marriages are still widely accepted. Young people believe their parents want their happiness and will choose wisely for them. But no one should be made to marry against their will. The marriage is a contract between the groom and the bride's father. The groom promises to provide for and protect his wife.

Divorce

Divorce is allowed in Islam but was regarded by Muhammad as 'the most hateful of permitted things'. If a divorce takes place the woman keeps all the household possessions. The husband keeps and must support his children. The wife should be supported by her male relatives.

A bride and groom on their wedding day in India. Different Muslim countries have different wedding customs.

26

A mother and her daughters studying the Qur'an at home.

Fathers, mothers and children

In a Muslim family, the father is the head of the household. His main duty is to protect and provide for the family. The main task of the mother is to create a happy home and look after the children.

'Paradise is to be found at your mother's feet.'
Saying of the Prophet Muhammad

Both parents are expected to teach their children how to pray and fast. Young people are required to respect the old and to take care of them. Just as parents care and provide for children when they are young, so the children when they grow up should look after their parents as they grow old.

Muslim women are required to dress decently, keeping legs and arms covered in public. In many countries they also cover their hair or wear a veil.

Muslim women at prayer outside a mosque. Muslim men and women pray separately.

A MUSLIM LIFE

ABOUT A FIFTH OF THE WORLD'S POPULATION – 1,000 million people – are followers of Islam. Islam is the world's fastest growing faith, adding some 25 million new followers a year.

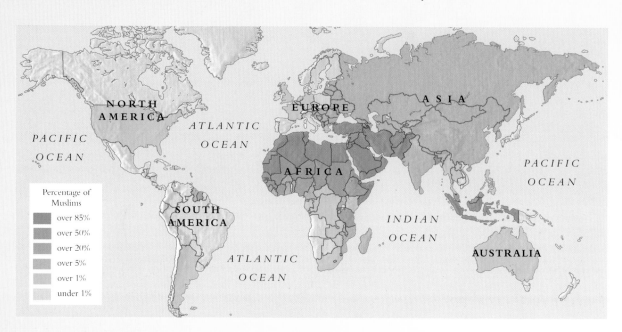

Percentage of Muslims
- over 85%
- over 50%
- over 20%
- over 5%
- over 1%
- under 1%

This map shows the percentage of Muslims in countries around the world.

Muslims on the move

Migration has brought many Muslims to western countries in search of work. In France the Muslims are mostly Arabs from North Africa, in Germany, they are Turks, and in the Netherlands, Indonesians. In Britain, most Muslims come from Bangladesh, Pakistan and India, but there are also others from Yemen, Nigeria, Malaysia, Turkey and the Middle East. Many now are British by birth. Most Muslims in the US are either Arabs from the Middle East, or American converts to Islam.

A religion to live by

Muslims regard their religion as a din – a complete way of life. Religion, for a Muslim, is not a separate matter between public and private life.

Religion involves belief, prayer, zakat, fasting and pilgrimage. But it also means carrying out one's duties as a member of a family and a community. The Prophet Muhammad's life provides Muslims with a model for morals and manners, at work, at home and in their dealings with others.

The family is the core of Muslim life. Here, a family prays together before a meal.

Individual and community

Each individual Muslim is responsible for his or her own life, but life is lived with other people. One may pray alone, but the Hadith stresses that it is better to pray with others. The pilgrimage to Makkah is the greatest single gathering of people on the face of the earth. It symbolizes the desire of Muslims to express their unity and show their willingness to sacrifice time and expense obeying Allah. When they return home, the hajjis, wherever they are, will turn towards Makkah to pray – and know that their Muslim brothers and sisters throughout the world will be doing the very same thing.

Hundreds of Chinese Muslims pray together. The Prophet strongly encouraged Muslims to pray together.

IMPORTANT DATES

Muslims do not use the term AD (Anno Domini – Year of Our Lord) because they do not think of Jesus as Lord. These dates are called CE – Common Era. Muslims also use a different calendar from the international calendar. It starts in 622CE when the Prophet Muhammad went to Madinah.

570 The Prophet Muhammad is born in the Arabian trading city of Makkah. The early death of his father and mother means that he is brought up first by his grandfather and then by his uncle Abu Talib.

610 The Prophet Muhammad receives his first revelation from Allah through the angel Jibril while meditating in a cave on Mount Hira outside Makkah.

613 The Prophet Muhammad begins preaching and wins converts among his own family and the poor.

622 The Prophet Muhammad and his followers emigrate from Makkah to the oasis of Madinah. This event, called the Hijra, marks 'the breaking of ties' between the Muslims and the people of Makkah. The first community of Muslims is established at Madinah. The Hijra also marks the beginning of the Islamic calendar.

624 Muslims defeat the people of Makkah at the battle of Badr. A revelation from Allah leads the Prophet Muhammad to order the Muslims to pray in the direction of Makkah, rather than towards Jerusalem as they had previously.

627 The people of Makkah defeat the Muslims at the battle of Uhud. The Prophet Muhammad warns the Muslims that this is a test of their faith.

630 The Muslims capture Makkah almost without a fight. The Prophet Muhammad clears the idols from the shrine of the Ka'aba.

632 The Prophet Muhammad dies.

632–4 Abu Bakr, the Prophet Muhammad's father-in-law, rules the Muslims as Khalifa and sends expeditions to force Arab tribes who have given up Islam to return to the faith.

634–44 Khalifa Umar rules. He continues to expand Islamic rule.

644–56 Khalifa Uthman rules. He continues Muslim expansion and orders the compilation of an edition of the Qur'an.

656–61 Khalifa Ali, son-in-law of the Prophet Muhammad, rules. After his death, his supporters (Shi'at Ali – the party of Ali, or Shiites) claim that only descendants of the Prophet Muhammad can be Khalifa.

661 Mu'awiya I seizes power on behalf of the Umayyad family and moves the capital of the Islamic realm to Damascus in Syria.

711-716 Muslim armies conquer Spain and Portugal

750 Umayyad rule is overthrown by the Abbasids, who claim descent from the Prophet Muhammad's uncle Abbas. A surviving Umayyad prince flees to Spain and becomes an independent Khalifa there.

758-762 A brand new capital is built at Baghdad in Iraq for the Abbasids.

1258 The Mongols sack Baghdad, ending Abbasid rule.

c.1300 The Turkish frontier fighter Osman begins conquering territory from the Christian empire of Byzantium, founding what will become the Ottoman empire.

1453 The Ottomans capture the Byzantine capital, Constantinople, and rename it Istanbul.

1492 Christian armies conquer Granada, ending seven centuries of Muslim rule in Spain.

1526 Babur ('Tiger'), an Afghan Muslim descended from the Mongols, conquers northern India to found the Mughal empire there. Mughal power declines after the reign of Aurangzeb (1658-1707) and is finally ended by the British in 1858. Islam remains one of the main faiths of India.

1529 Ottoman armies conquer the Balkans.

1924 Following its defeat in World War I the Ottoman Empire is ended and replaced by the Turkish Republic. Turkey introduces non-Muslim education and law but most Turks remain Muslim.

1925 Reza Shah Pahlavi, a soldier, takes power in Iran (Persia) and copies Turkey's reforms.

1979 An Islamic revolution in Iran overthrows the Pahlavis in favour of Shiite leaders.

GLOSSARY

Circumcise To cut off the foreskin of the penis. All Muslim males are circumcised.

Convert A person who decides to give up following one religion and begins to follow a new one.

Din A religion which is a complete way of life, not just a matter of beliefs and ceremonies.

Divine Being like Allah, godlike. Words that are divine are ones that come from Allah.

Eternal Lasting for ever.

Fast To give up eating or drinking. The month-long fast of Ramadan is one of the Five Pillars of Islam.

Hadith The record of the words and deeds of the Prophet Muhammad. Hadith is an important source of laws and guidance for Muslims.

Hafiz Someone who knows the entire Qur'an by heart. Often a blind Muslim will become a hafiz and earn a living by reciting on public occasions.

Hajj The pilgrimage to Makkah. It is one of the Five Pillars of Islam.

Hajji/Hajjah The title of a man or a woman who has made the pilgrimage to Makkah.

Halal Permitted. Halal meat is meat from an animal that has been slaughtered in the approved manner.

Haram Forbidden. Alcohol, drugs and certain meats are haram.

Hijra Migration or departure, as when the Prophet Muhammad left Makkah for Madinah in 622.

Ihram A hajji's state of purity.

Imam The leader of Islamic prayer in a mosque.

Khalifa Caliph. This literally means 'successor' and was the title taken by Abu Bakr and those who followed him as head of the community of Muslims. They succeeded to the Prophet Muhammad's position as ruler but did not claim to be prophets.

Meditate To become calm and control one's thoughts.

Mihrab The mark or niche on the wall of a mosque indicating the direction of Makkah – the direction in which worshippers pray.

Minaret The tower on a mosque, traditionally used for the muezzin's call to prayer.

Minbar Pulpit from which the imam preaches a sermon on Friday.

Muezzin The person who calls Muslims to prayer.

Niyyah Declaration of an intention. Muslims declare their intention to pray or go on a pilgrimage to show that they are thinking about what they are doing.

Pilgrimage A journey for a religious purpose.

Prophet A teacher inspired by Allah.

Rak'ah Set series of actions and words of prayer used by Muslims in worship.

Revelation Important knowledge uncovered in a message from Allah.

Ritual An action or ceremony which symbolizes a belief or event.

Sacrifice To kill an animal for a religious purpose.

Salah Formal Islamic prayer, said in Arabic.

Sawm Fasting.

Shahadah The basic declaration of faith in Islam, *'I witness that there is no god but Allah and that Muhammad is the Prophet of Allah.'*

Shi'a Short for Shi'at Ali (party of Ali); Shiite Muslims believe that only Ali, the son-in-law of the Prophet, and his descendants had the right to become Khalifa and should be revered.

Sunna The model behaviour established by the words and deeds of the Prophet Muhammad.

Sunni A follower of the Sunna; the majority (about 85–90 per cent) of Muslims are Sunni.

Surah Literally 'row'; a chapter of the Qur'an.

Ummah The global community of Muslims.

Wudu Washing before prayer.

Zakat Giving money to charity as required as a duty of Islam. The amount is calculated according to a person's surplus wealth, after what they need for their family and to carry on their business has been allowed for.

INDEX